GEOMANTIC

First published in 2016 by
The Dedalus Press
13 Moyclare Road
Baldoyle
Dublin 13
Ireland

www.**dedaluspress**.com

ISBN 978 1 910251 15 7 paperback
ISBN 978 1 910251 16 4 hardback

Dedalus Press titles are represented in the UK by
NBN International, Airport Business Centre (ABC)
10 Thornbury Road, Plymouth PL6 7P, UK,
and in North America by Syracuse University Press, Inc.,
621 Skytop Road, Suite 110, Syracuse, New York 13244.

Cover image by Paula Meehan

The Dedalus Press receives financial assistance from
The Arts Council / An Chomhairle Ealaíon

GEOMANTIC

Paula Meehan

DEDALUS PRESS

DUBLIN, IRELAND

Contents

Indefatigable dazzling / terrestrial strangeness.
 – Ciaran Carson

for
Ciaran Carson & Deirdre Shannon

GEOMANTIC

The Moons

Moons like petals adrift on the stream:
night moon and day moon, moon in eclipse,
slender new moon in the winter sky,
and full harvest moon — a golden ball;
moon of my first breath, my mother's death,
grandfather moon, my father's frail boat,
moon of my lost child, my sister's fall,
moon of my belovèd's waking dream,
moons of my life adrift on the stream.

The Patternings

I sketch the patternings of the sea:
the iter- and reiteration
of event. Similar; not the same.

Lulled by dull predictability
of my own selves' dreary projections,
I've confused the sacred with its name.

Better scan fractals, rhyme sea with tree,
tune into tantric syncopation
my mortal gods, frantic and profane.

The Trust

Leave her in the lap of Our Lady —
her counsel for where to place the lost
when we close the door on their madness.
She slammed the door on her own daughter,
left her to the city's chartered streets,
found her in the Liffey's dark water,
cast up in the week before Christmas,
the city gripped in the hardest frost
the eve of the new austerity.

The Conjuration

I walked your ghost trail through the city,
I knocked at all the old addresses,
but nowhere did I find word of you.
One friend said you'd died. It was a lie:
I knew by the shadows in her eyes.
She swore you'd been some class of a spy.
I was but one in a lengthening queue
of women crazed by your excesses,
fucking fools who deserved no pity.

The Rub

It was what she'd say when things got rough
back there in Thebes Central — the kitchen —
where it never came out in the wash,
the one original stain, the sin
of the fathers spun down through the years.
Every word she hurled could pierce the skin:
she could talk common, she could talk posh.
I sat like a stone growing lichen.
What didn't kill me would make me tough.

The Grimoire

When you call it my book of shadows
I scry the tawny deer move upwind
towards the Furry Glen, and the stars
above have their own kind of grammar,
their own declension of wingèd folk —
the Mother, the Father, the Other.
I understand the transit of Mars
is a fated course that has us twinned
lost souls beneath the skylight window.

The Row

No matter what you tell me tonight
about the lost republic, about
the last chance, the last hope, the last toss
of the coin, the flipside, the B-side,
the be all and end all of nothing,
everything you say will be unsaid
by morning; and we've borne too much loss
between us to waste our time in doubt
composing cruel censorious slights.

The Querant

There's nothing to be learned from the rain
falling through red, through green neon light,
nothing to be gleaned on the matter,

no solace in the sound of the train
shunting you home in the dark of night.
Under streetlamps the old boys gather

to talk of the old country, its pain.
Their childhoods dying in their hindsight,
with the smell of their fields in summer.

The Fear

Circling round the work for hours afraid
of what I might say or fail to say,
the song unmade, last night's dream betrayed,
I wander through the rooms: the rain,
which has drenched the unkempt streets for days,
beats a loud tattoo upon the pane
then stops of a sudden. The stanzas
open up to the sun's healing rays
answering my prayers — this mantra!

The Clouds

Some mornings the room is full of clouds,
clouds where the students' heads ought be,
little weather systems of their own.

They put all their work up on the cloud:
dream and song and secret and story.
Consciousness seeds the digital zone

with cold fronts, sunny spells, cirrus clouds.
Every weather of the room I grieve
the cloud children of the new machines.

The Last Lesson

Romantic, geomantic, antic:
the small green fields, the earth from above,
the autumn hedgerows, turning, turning,
turned with winter's white and black magic
into hieroglyphs of mortal love
signaling heaven with our yearning.
The frail glider suddenly mythic
is stopped a moment as if to prove
the craft is lighter than the learning.

The Feathers

To be so far up riding thermals
a summer's morning in early May
is to enter the realm of the hawk

or light-born wingèd creature, angel
with a thunderclap come out to play
in the wave lift —
                                    while below we walk

the sad road of the earthbound carnal
who dream flight, who scan the milky way
and turn the sky blue with crazy talk.

The Memory Stick

I searched high, low, all over the place
growing more anxious by the minute:
a whole summer's work in a square inch
cohesion of metal and plastic —
an ode, an elegy, a ballad,
a sonnet flawed by its rhetoric
but still retrievable at a pinch,
if I could recall where I put it,
the memory stick in its shiny case.

The Fascinator

I tracked her through the marketplace by
the feathered contraption on her head.
She told me it was from the Latin
fascinare: to spellbind, or to cast
a spell, but I saw the rods, the axe,
the threads that bind us tight to the past.
Suddenly: early morning matins
drowning out the words best left unsaid,
minims rising to the empty sky.

The Pinhead

Just how many angels were dancing
last night in your junk-dazed eyes? And how
in god's name, can you be such a drag

on this miraculous, entrancing
creation? You swear you can change now.
With your life in a black plastic bag:

we dread the sight of you — advancing
feathers flying, thunder on your brow,
frightening the children, and the dog.

The Spank

That time his grandmother sat me down
with sad news of a daughter's child
who'd turned to *spank* and who'd have thought it
of a boy so beautiful and smart?

Good family, everything to live for.

In the winter dusk, a heart to heart:
did I know where, from whom he bought it?
I'd seen him — sometimes meek, sometimes wild,
hustling for smack in his tarnished crown.

The Bird

O what can ail thee, little green bird,
singing your heart out this winter dawn?
From which suburban house have you fled,
plucky canary freed of your cage?
A murder of crows from the high pines
rejects your approach with raucous rage.
Gentle other, soon you'll be stone dead,
tangled feathers on the frosty lawn,
fallen angel in a fallen world.

The Gift

My godmother on her deathbed gave
up this memory of me aged two
in my grandmother Mary's garden
about the time I first got language.
Like a queen who rules all she surveys
I'm saying *nice nice nice* as I wave
to bee, fly, worm, wasp, bird, to the blue
cloudless sky, at home in creation,
my realm bordered by sweet privet hedge.

The Hide

This morning the white wash on the line
like prayer flags filling; then spilling
the wind onto the shadows below!

How thin, how vulnerable the skin
at wrist, temple, sole, throat, groin: the tongue
licks a secret path to the earlobe

and whispers to the creature within
the darkening words of an old song
while childhood ghosts buffet the window.

The Old Neighbourhood

I was dreaming of Gardiner Street
again, Georgian inner cityscape —
how they named it when they laid it out
somewhat like a natal horoscope,
squares that trine and sextile country seats.

As if summoned on some psychic skype
the ghosts of my childhood manifest,
my feral girls, my angels, who skipt
summer into being with each beat.

The Boy from the Gloucester Diamond

What did we know of bogs? Their beauty?
The names of their flowers? Their wild skies?

We cursed those cold black-robed men who swept
the four winds and the four known seasons
out heaven's door down on us below.
They were beyond all sense, all reason.

By an unmarked grave we knelt and wept,
spoke of his head of curls, his green eyes,
his broken back. His small hands empty.

The Cardboard Suitcase

All he brought was his native city,
its jade green river, its streetsellers' cries,
hooves on cobbles, feral cats who crept
the grimy docks, old men with pigeons
whistling up winds, his granny's window,
the yard below, his mother's apron,
his sister's handbag — its smell. He slept
beyond reach of the fists, the lies.
He dreamt beyond reach of our pity.

The Understanding

I heard the kids in the back garden,
their grandfather's last day in the house,
his good blue suitcase parked in the hall.

— Da told Mr. Burke he's a goner:
    he's definitely not coming back home.

— Ma said he might if he gets better;
    he'll get lots of injections and all.

— Yeah right. It's like the place they sent Rex.
    It's where they put the old people down.

The Last Thing

my ebbing father said to me was
not the wind before he slipped below
the horizon of his morphine dream.

So was it the moon in the hospice
rigging? Or the cloud's buoyant shadow?
Or my mother's voice helming him home?

No. I think it was some ferocious
wingèd creature at the ward's window
breast feathers flecked with salt-laced foam.

The Street

with only one tree was from a dream
of a city where I'd lost my mind
on a bright May morning that broken year,
and every soul passing my window

into the heart of their own mysteries

took a piece of me away with them,
their eyes confiding a double bind
that left me void, that tuned my ear
to woodwind in a summer hedgerow.

The Promise

I won't do it. Not today, I won't
do it, anyway. Not today. No.
Not because I can't do it. I won't.
Fallow fields lie dreaming under snow:
they won't be ploughed. Not this spring they won't.
On the fencepost, a grey hooded crow
is part of some mystery I won't
fathom now. Though I'm really quite low,
I won't do it. Not today. I won't.

The Syllables

Only the library angel knew
in which holy books the seeds were hid
that year they started cutting the tongues
out of the heads of the blasphemers.
One girl, a virgin, made a plain chant:
all those who heard took solace and drew
close; and we who can still speak are bid
sing it out at the top of our lungs,
seed syllables of the earth's dreamers.

The Poet

after Rilke

No belovèd, no home to go to,
no place on this earth where I can stand
and call myself citizen. Alone
in the face of these days, these long nights,
each moment a bird that flies from me.
With empty hands I enter the light
of each creature, each flower, each stone;
my spirit incarnate bears the wound
of knowing, the price of making do.

The Moon Rose Over an Open Field

Count the syllables, a perfect line:
the way moon rises with the vowels,
the knacky way it moves on the tongue
and beats out its intent on the ear.
When I heard it first my fate was sealed:
it offered a pathway out of fear,
order from chaos when I was young,
a pure lyric from inchoate growls,
muse magic wrought from the power of nine.

The Godling

The downy ones over his breastbone
are the feathers I need to ruffle.
His fathomless eyes follow me round
the garden; he perches on my spade
and looks into the depths of the grave
I have patiently and neatly made.
He emits a sycophantic sound
striding through the morning's kerfuffle,
chiding me and my waning hormones.

The Melter

I remember you well in Grogan's.
You called it the Poet's Horror Hole.
And though it was easy to get there,
it was harder to find a way home.
Now that you're on the straight and narrow
with your charts, your mottoes, your slogans,
your strategies, your game plans, your goals
you're melting our heads with disasters,
with gossip, with lost-bar-god syndrome.

The Witch's Tit

that I was suckled at, those beestings —
part Dublin, part Cork — wholly imbued
with notions of first and second place.

Who deserves a seat at the feastings?
Who gets leavings? Crumbs? Old bones well chewed?
I could never look her in the face,

tit for tat, without hearing these things:
pig, cunt, bitch, signal to her lewd,
kitschy, alcoholic fall from grace.

The Mother Tongue

Was it beaten into me or out
of me? Is it the lump in my throat
where words clot and snag and block the glut

that builds and builds and threatens to blow
my head off? Though there's no word for no,
grant me the words for grey hooded crow,

apple orchard, child, tenement, slut,
caravel, quinquireme, black-sailed boat,
the far shining cities of the south.

The Poetry

Was it beaten into me or out
of me? The ur question, always doubt.

Never certainty, never sure the song
is on the right track. I've got it wrong

so often, failure is a true friend

of my long night's journey into day.
My gibbering ghosts must have their say:

Mother, Teacher, Lost Child, will not cease
until dawn breaks through in brutal peace.

The Book from Belfast

That day I thought I'd never find peace
or draw a sane breath this side of Hell,
the postman knocked with Berenson's tome:
Italian Painters of the Renaissance.
I couldn't read; typeface made me ill;
when I closed my sore eyes I would dream
witchsniffing burners from Aberdeen.
So then, your gift salvific — the grace
of childhood, all halo, wing, animal.

The Bonnet

That Samhain we dressed as characters
        from *Persuasion:* we gender-bended
through the Finglas fields. I wore velvet
        trousers and cravat. You pranced about
in a bonnet nicknamed Jane Austen:
        golden straw sprigged with silk columbine.

By the time we sat summer exams
        you were wasted. We read in your eyes
the opened grave, the funeral rain.

The Broken Bough

We held our breath when you were a boy
out on a limb of the old oak tree,
helpless below as you shimmied up
into its shadowy canopy.
That day the bough broke and you clung there
alone through the sudden thunderstorm.
We came upon you after unafraid
though drenched to the bone.

                    The pattern set:
all those times since, we wasted our breath.

The Lists

My list: candles, flowers, bulbs, butter,
a ream of copy paper, red pen,
red wine, something for Tracy's baby.

Your list: note for Johnny, note for Ma,
plastic sheeting, chair, six feet of rope.

I got the word in The Square, Tallaght,
by newborn layettes, pink and frilly,
your mother's voice sobbing down the line,
calling your name, over and over.

The Fever

Had I been sleeping I would have missed
the seagull at my sickbed window.
Just when I wondered was there something
stronger in the house to take away
my pain, I was lifted out of it
to soar above the square in the dark
on the seagull's salty myth-flecked wings,
to navigate by stars, to follow
to the bitter end the fated tryst.

The Outbreak

I was by the fruit and vegetables
when I heard that war had broken out.

The vividity of a sudden
of all things in reach, in sight, in how

each upturned face was rendered sacred.

And in that moment I made a vow
that I would not let my heart harden

though all I valued be put to rout
by their betrayals, their reprisals.

The Luck

I don't do the past, said my father,
into my oldfashioned microphone.
The rain, the eternal Irish rain,
beats and beats and beats at the window
and the fattening geese are dreaming
of the north. I knew that he'd be dead
by Samhain when the geese returned again.
We bet online and watched the horses,
all going round the bend together.

The Pearl

My mother did nothing but the past,
over and over. Sifting the grains
for the one minuscule speck around
      which all of her grief accreted to pearl.
Historical grit — the first gunshot
      or first tricolour hoisted over
the G.P.O. that Easter lunchtime,
or a secret memory handed down,
toxic in her lonely heart of hearts.

The Child I Was

Nineteen sixty-six, eleven years
       old, let me die for Ireland I prayed,
Sword of Light in my grubby hand, though
       I thought the O'Connell Monument
was all about the wingèd women
       at its base, and when Nelson was blown
off his Pillar my Dublin sky wept.
       I understood we were poor — we lived
on streets named for the patriot dead.

The Commemorations Take Our Minds
Off the Now

A boon to the Government; they rule
      in the knowledge that none can keep track
of just how much of the country has
been flogged like an old nag to within
an inch of its life. The karmic wheel
      goes round and round. I commemorate
the poor going round and round the bend.
      How mad do you have to be to make
sense of the state of the State we're in?

The Graves at Arbour Hill

We all die for Ireland in the end,
        whether sooner or later. I'll die
myself for Ireland one of the days.
        And even though I've lived for Ireland
with every breath of my being,
        with each and every beat of my heart,
there'll come a day I'll be dust in wind,
        Irish dust in Irish wind, a hundred
and a hundred million years from now.

The Peace

Peace will come: let it begin with me.

Slogan from my wild and misspent youth,
comes back each time I practice Tai Chi,
when I meditate on the Seven,
      the Holy Seven Signatories.
I *Part the Horse's Mane*, I *Wave Hands*
      Like Clouds, I am a *White Crane Spreading
Her Wings.* When I *Grasp the Swallow's Tail,*
      I might undo the State's betrayal:
redemption through mastery of form.

The Clue

I don't do the past, said my father
and turned back to his crossword puzzle:
three down 'sold out' eight letters — *betrayed*
'essential to life' five letters — *water*
'flag of the people'— *the starry plough.*

The seven stars on a field of blue —
dream of a republic, dream of hope.

Flowering on the island every spring,
stars and dreams: the natal horoscope.

The Singer

You are the gifted one, you are pure
joy in the morning early, you are
our broken hearts when night has come on
and the moon is full in the river
where the road winds down to the harbour:
a woman picks up a fountain pen,
writes a farewell note to her lover,
a note she'll rewrite then abandon
before your canticle is over.

The Hands

Today I got my old woman's hands.
I laid my young woman's hands away
in the drawer with my young woman's hair,
that thick dark braid that hung to my waist.
Mind how he swung me once round and round
the garden, to Sergeant Pepper's Band.
That was long ago, a wedding day.
The ring is lost; lost are all my cares.
Old woman's hands now, old woman's face.

The Recipe

She believed it would strengthen the blood,
the soup my grandmother Mary made:
nettle, onion, parsley, thyme and spud —

each spring when the nettle tips appeared
in clumps the rough end of the back yard.
I, a willing and complicit ward,

dogged her footsteps. Thus to learn the hard
way what a nettle was, to learn that good
comes sleeved in pain, had best be suffered.

The May Altar, 58 Collins Avenue, Killester

You dressed it with lilac and privet,
the good crystal vase on white linen,
wax candles, bright medals, hymn singing
to Stella Maris, Star of the Sea.

You prayed to Our Lady to mind you.
You believed in angels and mercy.

As if heaven wept at your going
it rained the whole day you left Dublin,
rained on the girl you were, setting out.

The Offering

To kneel at the altar of memory,
to offer up what fragments we can
of the mystery that is your death.

Your life we are fated to carry
into each beautiful new morning
like emigrants safely come to land

after a rough crossing, their first breath
ashore — O sweet angel of mercy,
star of the wanderer, child of the sea.

The Beauty (Of It)

Northside graffiti of a morning,
acid colours along the train line,
suburban trippers out the window,

elders and the unemployed dreaming,
radiant in the winter sunshine
as if we believe both friend and foe

are tucked up safe from harm and sleeping
when we lift our eyes to the mountains
golden in their coverlet of snow.

The Web

i giorni della merla

I spun those nights to Van Morrison
on Fitzroy Avenue in a dream
part Victoriana, part nightmare.
Elsewhere, at my web's frayed selvage,
you were dying, less yourself each day
in a white cancer ward in Dublin.
I scanned your memory for this meme:
that time you talked me down, pulled me clear
of my fevered visions, my blank page.

The Great Poet

That strange full-on proliferation
of verse after the great poet died,
as if a peerless diamond shattered
into smithereens and each facet
mirrored to infinity our dream
of perfect balance, integration.

We wrought newfangled order, implied
in patterns symmetric, then scattered:
fractals logarithmic and drastic.

The Age of Embrocations and Naps

can only be a matter of time:
this morning's blast of wintergreen
where once the scent of ylang ylang
permeated our chest of drawers.
A woman I hardly recognise
flits from mirror to mirror; older
and wiser, she speaks in a sing-song
voice which lulls us both to clearer dreams,
spooled snugly on her cold craft of rhyme.

The Old Professor

It's not just that he can't remember
you: he can't recall any of it:
the university, his other
students. I rocked. I reeled. I was knocked
off kilter, as if the child in me
had stepped up to the blackboard and picked
up the chalky duster and wiped her
future lines away, even the bit
where he helps me get sober and clear.

The January Bee

who comes to the winter-flowering shrub,
grief in his empty pouches, who sups
alone in the stilled garden this dusk:

I would have missed him only I stopped
mid-argument to watch the moonrise
over the wet roofs of the suburb

and caught him at work deep in the musk,
shaking the bells of the scarce blossoms,
tolling our angers, ringing in peace.

The Hexagram

Before starting, find the lines — broken
and whole — arranged as a hexagram;
the crescent moon waxing, a token

in the night sky of beginnings. Palms
open to the grace of what might fall
like snow to the snow-white page. How calm

I am, and cool, when I hear the call.
She has found me out, in my silence,
come with rumours of heaven, of hell.

The Struggle

In my garden — teasel, nettle, thistle,
taken hold since I lifted my hand;
with thorn, sting, clawed hooks they do battle

bristling towards the ruin of my house.
Like poetry — territorial
and patient. Humble only to bees;

flowering to them, opening to them,
and how, against winter's unleaved trees,
they scribe grace note, quaver, minim.

The Thaw

I watch a she-wolf treading thin ice
beyond the birches. I hold my breath —
muffled river music. Lost balance

and the wolf stumbles, skirts death,
jumps to the bank just as the ice cracks,
her shadow snagged by water. Beneath

the trees, snowdrops measure the exact
shift in light that ends the long winter —
and out there on the snowfield, her tracks.

The Leningrad Muse

What cracked the ice, what broke the silence?
Groans of prisoners. After thunder,
church bells pealing. Out of the violence

her voice clear above mocking laughter.
Flute music then and her frantic dance;
on the east wind news of fresh torture.

Drumbeat. Heartbeat. Edge of edge of chance.
She moves through me: mother and daughter,
ancient lover. She works me to trance.

The Line

I find the line. I lose it. I find
the line again. I turn it over
and feel it move through ear, heart, mind,

tracking the prints back to the den's mouth
beside a frozen lake, beneath trees
where again I'm fated to give birth.

Blood on my tongue, her pelt licked and eased
from nose to tip of tail. The black earth
under snow yearning for tender green.

The New Regime

After love we sleep curled together.
I am dreaming her old dreams; she dreams
pines freighted with snow, ice storm weather.

Her mouth's rimed with my milk, her hair streams
in curls and rivulets down her back.
She is spelling out the new regime:

its ins, its outs, my place in the pack;
where she keeps the names of the lost things;
how to bear the pain, the sweats, the rack.

The Withdrawal

Strung out again I stumble through nights
without her. Cold grey street. Hot grey sheet.
Body drab as lead, I shun the light.

She has shown me what it's like to die.
Bereft, out of favour, I won't write
one syllable of truth, one good lie.

I crave her cool comfort, her deep shade.
She's busy elsewhere despite how I try
to lure her back with this song I've made.

The Hempen Rope

And thus I turn what she has given.
I offer it up to them in hope,
in despair, part wasted, part shriven,

I have twisted my own hempen rope
with those sad listeners as witness.
Though I know nothing of how they cope

in their real, their secret lives, I bless
them in their every generation
in their devotions, in their duress.

The Contract

From the fret of insomnia some
cold lines on a page; a candle
gutters on the windowsill. Oh come

morning bells, call me back to myself,
call sinner and saint to watch snow fall
on the city, the forest, the wolf

tracking her cub the length of the lake.
Before this moon clears the horizon
I'll give whatever she needs to take.

The Poem for Dillon with North Carolina in It

After the slammed doors the door opening
to my broken face; and the window
that gave onto darkness engulfing
your humid subtropical biome.
Red fox and red wolf and white-tailed deer.
Cornsnake, milksnake, diamond back rattler,
the copperhead you taught me to fear —
they slither through memory's field: rare,
heraldic, set now and fixed in print.

The Black Kite

the children fly over Burrow Beach
this August morning

                — (like the black sails
Aegeus saw bearing on Athens
portending grief and the fall of his house,
or like Victorian widows' weeds,
an incongruity of black bows) —

which by a sudden squall is taken
struggling out to sea. When it fails
and falls, it falls far beyond our reach.

The Ghost Song

"The singers and workers that never handled the air"
— Gwendolyn Brooks

From a dream of summer, of absinthe,
I woke to winter. Carol singers
decked the halls of some long-lost homeland.
Late-night shoppers and drowsy workers
headed for the train.
                    So the night that
you died was two-faced, June light never
far from mind though snow fell. I handled
grief like molten sunshine, learned to breathe
your high lithe ghost song from thinnest air.

The Inscription

'Honour the dust ...' wrote Gary Snyder
in my old copy of *No Nature*
before Bella, our belovèd dog,
got her teeth into it. Now dog-eared,
oft-thumbed, much annotated, it sits
on a bockety shelf right beside
the well-made box wherein lies her wag,
her bark, her growl, her lick, her rapture
of devotion — her dust we honour.

The Storm

When we first met, the hedgerows were white
with blackthorn blossom. Nineteen ninety:
the February storm that brought down

the ancient oaks and shook the rafters,
that grounded planes, that closed all the ports,
picked us up and threw us together.

Like refugees newly come to town
we made a stern language of beauty
all spring into the summer's stretched light.

The Blues

In moonlight the landscape was all blue —
frit of cobalt, french ultramarine,
far-off hills of phtalocyanine
and that gleam of light on lake water
cerulean, shore rocks indigo,
fugitive soldiers freezing to death
on a Prussian ground — when my belovèd
turned on me his eyes of blue mercy:
lapis lazuli, pupils of gold.

The Flood

It was only when it receded
we knew it for the gift it had been.
If truth be told we missed the water.

It was exactly what we'd needed.
We missed the way it made a mirror —
doubled goose, godwit, egret, heron;

and that once in moonlight we looked down
on two complete and drowning strangers,
those depths where later wolfbane seeded.

The Woodpile

We worked our way through it log by log:
three winters' worth of heat, precious light
through the darkest nights, the darkest days.

You'd remarked you knew the very tree,
that last June you stacked them in the barn —
the silver logs in their fret of moss.

You must have had the news already,
whistling from the woodpile's finished height,
your arms about your favoured black dog.

The Quilt

It was a simple affair — nine squares
by nine squares, blue on green spots, stripes, bows
alternate with gold on red chevrons:
my grandmother's quilt I slept under
the long and winding nights of childhood.

Above the bed a roundy window:
my own full moon. I loved the weathers
wheeling past, the stars, the summer suns;
my aunties' deep breaths, distant thunder.

The Food Chain

I could eat the moon, the breaking waves,
the moonlight sifting through the pine trees;
I could eat you, my beauty, your gaze

following that scrawny village cat
who stalks the plump frog who stalks the bug
who labours over the hessian mat

while we eat little silver fishes
and are nibbled on in turn by flies
glazed by the shine of this blood moon's rise.

The Road to Agios Kirikos

I imagine our ghosts hand in hand,
the full May moon overhead, the smell
of oregano, of thyme, of sage;

I imagine they'll pause at the wall
where the glow-worms between the stones
sing the stardust of which they're made.

They can ramble at their ease, they've all
the time in the world before the day
claims, from their bright souls, their dying minds.

The Handful of Earth

Under scrutiny it tells us all
we need to know about our futures,
it being composted of our past lives,
the nine years in this house by the sea.
Under the paths stars make, wild birds call.

I fancy I could read it like leaves
of tea, yarrow stalks thrown down, tarot,
its minutest narratives of grief,
its aboriginal patternings.

The Sea Cave

It is as close as I'll get to her
in this life: to swim into the dark
deep in the cave where the hot springs are,

to float in her amniotic dream
of children, of a husband, of home.
Flickers of light there where minnows teem

like memories pulsing through my veins,
that lull me, that shrive me, uncertain
whether I hear her heartbeat or mine.

The Island

At home again on Ikaria,
our own bee-loud glade. How this morning
hawks were hung in the still mountain air;
a snake slithered into the kitchen,
three feet of elegant fear; the cats,
those thin village cats, napped in sunlight;
and last night's owl, startled into flight,
has us unsettled and creaturely
ourselves, sweeping the sea-girth garden.

NOTES AND ACKNOWLEDGEMENTS

My gratitude to editors, broadcasters and curators who first published these poems in divers combinations and versions.

These include:

Leo Hallissey who asked for a contribution to the Letterfrack Poetry Trail. 'The Boy from the Gloucester Diamond' and 'The Cardboard Suitcase' are carved in wood and situated at the entrance to the graveyard wherein lie the remains of boys who died during their time at the Letterfrack Industrial School;

'The Feathers', 'The Last Lesson' and 'The Clouds' published in *The Lighter Craft,* eds. Chris Morash and Kevin Honan, a festschrift for Peter Denman, Maynooth, 2013;

'The Querant', 'The Pinhead' and 'The Conjuration' published in *Cyphers* 73, Spring 2014, eds. Leland Bardwell, Eiléan Ní Chuilleanáin and Macdara Woods;

'The Promise', 'The Pinhead', 'The Line', 'The Flood' and 'The Black Kite' were recorded for *Cyphers*, CD produced by Niall Woods, 2015;

'The Feathers', 'The Trust', 'The Blues', 'The Fascinator', 'The Last Lesson' and 'The Querant', in translation into Castilian by Fernando Toda Iglesia as 'Las plumas', 'La confianza', 'Azules', 'La fascinadora', 'La última lección' and 'Los que buscan', in *Zurgai,* ed. Pablo Gonzalez de Langarika, Bilbao, June, 2014;

'The Moon Rose Over an Open Field', this title derived from a line from 'America' a song written by Paul Simon, from the Simon & Garfunkel album, *Bookends,* Columbia Records, 1968;

'The Promise' was inspired by Cecily Brennan's sculpture 'Suicide Guards', two wrist protectors in cast stainless steel and velcro, with the words *don't do it* on one and *not today anyway* on the other, 2001;

'The Memory Stick' and 'The Flood' in *Berryman's Fate: Reception and Redress,* ed. Philip Coleman, Arlen House, 2015;

'The May Altar, 58 Collins Avenue, Killester' and 'The Offering' for Jacinta McCarthy's funeral mass, 26th of August 2014, St. Marychurch, Torquay, Devon;

'The Moons' in braille in *Verbal Sun: Poems,* eds. Philip Coleman and Diane Sadler, NCBI Publications, Dublin, 2016;

'The Moons' (in English with Galician translation) was also recorded by TREME (Su Garrido Pombo and Margarida Mariño) on their album *Mundo Ideal,* 2016;

'The Street', 'The Trust', 'The Rub' and 'The Promise' in *Dream of a City: Anthology of Contemporary Poetry* from *Limerick City of Culture 2014,* eds. Vivienne McKechnie and Kevin Honan, Astrolabe Press, 2014;

'The Last Thing' and 'The Hands' in *The SHOp,* 46/47 Autumn/Winter 2014, eds. Hilary and John Wakeman, Schull, Co. Cork;

'The Blues', 'The Patternings' and 'The Old Professor' in *Ploughshares: TransAtlantic All Poetry Issue,* Spring 2015, ed. Neil Astley, Emerson College, Boston;

'The Bonnet' in *All My Important Nothings,* ed. Maura Dooley, Smith/Doorstep, (The Poetry Business), Sheffield, 2015, to mark Maura Dooley's time as Poet-in-Residence at Jane Austen's home in Chawton, Hampshire;

'The Food Chain' in Ψ, ed. Pádraic Moore, and in Fokidos Project, Athens, also curated by Pádraic Moore, accompanied by a visual art work by Navine G. Khan-Dossos;

'The Hexagram', 'The Struggle', 'The Thaw', 'The Leningrad Muse', 'The Line', 'The New Regime', 'The Withdrawal', 'The

Hempen Rope' and 'The Contract', published as 'Mysteries of the Craft', in *The SHOp, 32,* Spring 2010, eds. Hilary and John Wakeman, Schull, Co. Cork. They are dedicated to Nuala Ní Dhomhnaill and were first presented at the Imram Féile 2007 with music by Jackie Leven;

'The Fever', 'The Lists', 'The Singer' and 'The Outbreak' in *Circle & Square,* ed. Eileen Casey, Fiery Arrow Press, Dublin, 2015;

'The Luck', 'The Pearl', 'The Child I Was', 'The Commemorations Take Our Minds Off the Now', 'The Graves at Arbour Hill', 'The Peace' and 'The Cure' form a sequence published as 'Doing the Past' in *16,* Stoney Road Press / An Post / Poetry Ireland, fine art edition; also Witness History exhibition in GPO, 2016; also *In Between Silence, where we really exist,* recorded and produced by Stano and Denise Dunphy, 2016;

'The Ghost Song' in *The Twelve Poems of Christmas* (Volume Seven), selected and introduced by Carol Ann Duffy, The Candlestick Press, Nottingham, U.K, 2015;

'The Ghost Song' also published in *The Golden Shovel: Honouring Gwendolyn Brooks,* ed. Peter Kahn, The University of Arkansas Press, Fayetteville, 2016;

'The January Bee' in *If Bees are Few: A Hive of Bee Poems,* ed. James Lenfestey, University of Minnesota Press, Minneapolis, 2016;

'The Book from Belfast' and 'The Grimoire' included in *Pax,* the sponsors' portfolio, Graphic Studio, Dublin, 2016, with prints by Grainne Cuffe, Sharon Lee, Mary Lohan and Tom Phelan;

'The Food Chain', 'The Road to Agios Kirikos' and 'The Sea Cave' in *The Ogham Stone,* Limerick University, Spring 2016;

'The Flood', 'The Trust', 'The Conjuration', 'The Grimoire' and 'The Melter' in *The Café Review,* ed. Steve Luttrell, Spring 2016;

'The Inscription' in *Cold Mountain Review,* ed. Kathryn Kirkpatrick, Appalacian State University, Boone, North Carolina, 2016;

'The Querant', 'The Pinhead', 'The Hide', 'The Old Neighbourhood', 'The Last Thing', 'The Promise', 'The Mother Tongue', 'The Poetry' and 'The Trust' in *Lacunae,* ed. Medb Ruane, 2016;

'The Quilt' in *All Through the Night: Lullabies and Night Poems,* ed. Marie Heaney, Poetry Ireland, Dublin, 2016.

ABOUT THE AUTHOR

Paula Meehan was born in Dublin where she still lives. She studied at Trinity College, Dublin, and at Eastern Washington University in the U.S. This is her seventh collection of poems. She has written plays for both adults and children, including *Cell* and *The Wolf of Winter*. *Music for Dogs: work for radio,* also published by Dedalus Press, collects three plays concerned with suicide during the economic boom years in Ireland. Her poetry has been translated into French, German, Galician, Italian, Japanese, Estonian, Spanish, Greek, Chinese and Irish. She has received the Butler Literary Award for Poetry presented by the Irish American Cultural Institute, the Marten Toonder Award for Literature, the Denis Devlin Award for *Dharmakaya,* published in 2000, the Lawrence O'Shaughnessy Award for Poetry 2015, and the PPI Award for Radio Drama. In 2013 Dedalus Press republished *Mysteries of the Home,* a selection of seminal poems from the 1980s and the 1990s. She was honoured with election to Aosdána, the Irish Academy for the Arts, in 1996. She was Ireland Professor of Poetry, 2013 – 2016, and her public lectures from these years, *Imaginary Bonnets with Real Bees in Them,* was published by UCD Press in 2016.